no ordinary DAYS

LITTLE EXERCISES TO
CHANGE EVERYTHING

WRITTEN BY M.H. CLARK · DESIGNED BY JILL LABIENIEC

What if there is no
such thing as
an ordinary day?

What if each day comes to you as vivid and rich and remarkable as anything you could ever hope for, and the secret is just to notice it all? To see the moments of magic, the places of potential, and the small, astonishing gifts.

This is a book about you. It's a book about the world. It's a book about surprising yourself in small ways, taking yourself just far enough from the things you know and expect so that you can see more, notice more, appreciate more.

These pages will inspire you to break with your ordinary habits long enough to let the light shine through. Long enough to see that this light is everywhere.

It's all a matter of paying attention, being awake in the present moment…

CHARLES DE LINT

When you sip your morning coffee or tea,

---

think about all the steps it has gone through to reach you. Think about the seeds being planted, the sun shining, the rain falling, all the time and all the people who have helped bring it to your cup. Try to taste the weather, the seasons, and all the human work that has gone into this one small thing.

*Take a moment to look
at your hands.
Observe them closely.*

These hands have been with you all
your life—working, making, and doing.
What precious things have these
hands held? Who have they touched?
What beautiful things have they
created? What are some things your
hands remember?

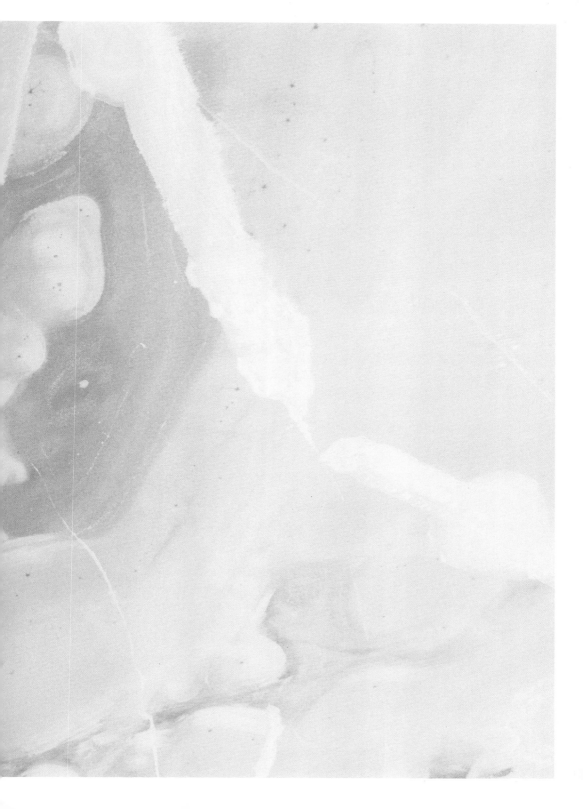

...make the ordinary come alive... The extraordinary will take care of itself.

WILLIAM MARTIN

Choose a tree you pass by every day.

Find a feeling you want to associate with that tree—gratitude, joy, calm, clearheadedness, groundedness, peace. Make it a point to notice this tree when you pass by it, and each time you do, connect to that feeling. Give it a moment to take root in you.

Go into a grocery store or florist and buy a bouquet of flowers that speaks to you.

It can be as simple or as extravagant as you like. Do this with the intention that you are going to find the perfect person to give this bouquet to—someone who needs a surprise gift or an unexpected delight. And when you leave the store, be on the lookout for them—a total stranger, an acquaintance, a friend. When you see them, you'll know.

Life is passing rapidly. Fiercely commit to every moment you find beautiful and remember it. Record it. Fully, wholeheartedly inhabit it.

VICTORIA ERICKSON

*Set the intention to find
one moment of
magic in every day.*

Allow it to be utterly simple or completely
profound—a corn muffin eaten over the kitchen
sink, the sunlight through the branches outside
your window, a text message at the perfect time.
When it happens, take note. Bookmark the page
of your day right there, so you can return as
often as you need.

Choose one stranger each day —

———————

someone you pass on the street, someone
you've never seen, someone you don't
know at all—and imagine something that
you share. Imagine a way that they are like
you—maybe something general, maybe
something specific. Maybe you share the
same favorite show, weekend hobby,
or secret aspiration. Maybe you had the
same thing for breakfast. If you catch
this person's eye, offer them a smile from
your place of shared connection.

*It's a constant, continuous, spectacular
world we live in. And every day
you see things that just knock you out,
if you pay attention.*

ROBERT IRWIN

The next time you're out under the night sky,

find a star to wish on. And make that wish with the same complete belief you had as a child—with a certainty that your belief can make a thing come true.

Write two short but specific thank you notes:

---

one to a friend, and one to yourself. Mail the first
one, and read the second one aloud to yourself.
Read it more than once. Read it until you don't feel
embarrassed anymore, but simply full of sincerity
and celebration.

*You have to live for the moment, each
and every day... the here, the now.*

SIMONE ELKELES

Find a picture of yourself as a child, and take a moment with it.

Look at your little face, your expression, the spirit that shines in your eyes. Offer yourself love, back through time, back through everything that has happened between that moment and right now. Love the child that you were, with your whole being. And then, wait for a moment, and allow the child that you were to send you love in return.

Choose a song
you haven't listened
to in years.

———————

Maybe it's one you listened to as a
teenager, or one that reminds you of
a first love, a road trip, a certain state of
mind. Play it without any distractions—
really listening, really honoring the part
of yourself that loved this music so
much. Who were you then? Where is
that part of you now?

...be all alive, body, soul,
mind, heart, spirit.

THOMAS MERTON

What's your internal weather?

Stormy? Overcast? Patches of sun? Do you like
the way you feel right now, or is it time for a new
weather system to come through? If you like
the weather that's there, hold on to it. And if not,
shift it—create a storm or a gust of wind to clear
out the old pattern and allow something new
to begin. Do this as often as you like until your
weather changes.

*Schedule an appointment
on your phone or
calendar for some time
this week.*

Just fifteen minutes. And when your alarm goes
off, do something unplanned and unexpected.
Do it away from a screen, and just for yourself—
whatever your heart is calling for. A walk outside,
a cup of coffee, an entry in your journal. Make
time for yourself. Make room for joy.

You have to see the miracles
for there to be miracles.

JANDY NELSON

Think of one thing in your life that you now have

---

that you once deeply wished for—it can be small or big, simple or profound—a home, a piece of furniture, an object, a person, a frame of mind. Have you forgotten how it felt to long for it? How does remembering how deeply you once wished for this change the way you feel about it now?

Try reframing your perspective on the things you have to do.

Start by choosing one thing a day, just one, that you "have" to do—something you feel neutral about, or maybe even slightly negatively, and reframe it as a thing you "get" to do. Maybe you "get" to go grocery shopping, or "get" to ride the train home. What does this language change for you? How do you feel differently about this task?

We can live only in the present.

S. N. GOENKA

Let go of something.

———————

Something you've been holding on to inside for a long while—something small, but something that surfaces from time to time and makes you feel embarrassed. It can be a thing you said, a thing you did, a thing you didn't do. Ask yourself if you can forgive yourself, and when you hear your own yes, imagine filling up a balloon with your embarrassment, holding it up, and letting it go.

Anchor yourself to a word for a while—

---

a word you want to feel more of, a word you
want to reach towards, or a word you want to
believe in. Write this word on a sticky note and
place it somewhere you'll see it often—your
computer monitor, your bathroom mirror, your
dashboard, above your kitchen sink. Live with
this word and let it seep its light into your days
until it's time to change it out for another one.

In this moment, there is plenty of time. In this moment, you are precisely as you should be. In this moment, there is infinite possibility.

VICTORIA MORAN

Dust yourself off before you come home.

———————

Imagine the work and people and distractions of the day wrapped around you like a coat and, before you put your key in the door, take that coat off. Imagine it falling to the floor, and let it stay there. Take a breath. And then, come home clean.

With special thanks to the entire Compendium family.

CREDITS:

Written by: M.H. Clark · Designed by: Jill Labieniec

Edited by: Amelia Riedler

Photography Credits:
Cover: Chuttersnap / Unsplash.com; pages 5, 58, 59: Chuttersnap / Unsplash.com; page 10: s11 / Photocase.com; pages 12, 13, 24, 25, 30: Aaron Burden / Unsplash.com; page 17: marshi / Photocase.com; page 18: deyangeorgiev / Photocase.com; page 22: Kristopher Roller / Unsplash.com; page 29: Jeremy Thomas / Unsplash.com; page 34: Clem Onojeghuo / Unsplash.com; pages 36, 37: Matt Howard / Unsplash.com; page 41: Andrew Bertram / Unsplash.com; page 42: Sweet Ice Cream Photography / Unsplash.com; page 46: Tänzerin (Eva Tenzer) / Photocase.com; pages 48, 49: Joel Filipe / Unsplash.com; page 53: Steffz / Photocase.com; page 54: Shannon McInnes / Unsplash.com

Library of Congress Control Number: 2017942873
ISBN: 978-1-943200-64-1

1st printing. Printed in China with soy inks.